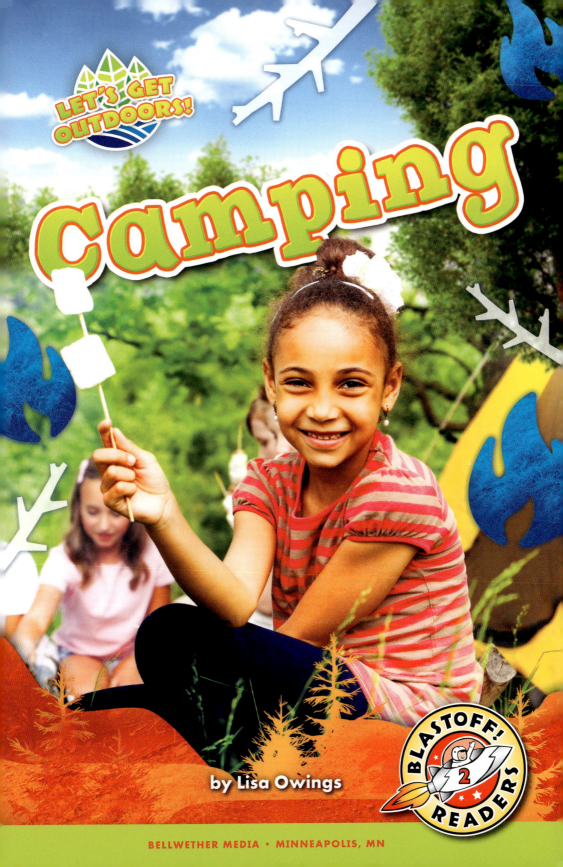

Blastoff! Readers are carefully developed by literacy experts to build reading stamina and move students toward fluency by combining standards-based content with developmentally appropriate text.

LEVELS

Level 1 provides the most support through repetition of high-frequency words, light text, predictable sentence patterns, and strong visual support.

Level 2 offers early readers a bit more challenge through varied sentences, increased text load, and text-supportive special features.

Level 3 advances early-fluent readers toward fluency through increased text load, less reliance on photos, advancing concepts, longer sentences, and more complex special features.

★ Blastoff! Universe

Reading Level

Grade K

Grades 1–3

Grade 4

This edition first published in 2023 by Bellwether Media, Inc.

No part of this publication may be reproduced in whole or in part without written permission of the publisher. For information regarding permission, write to Bellwether Media, Inc., Attention: Permissions Department, 6012 Blue Circle Drive, Minnetonka, MN 55343.

Library of Congress Cataloging-in-Publication Data

LC record for Camping available at: https://lccn.loc.gov/2022038739

Text copyright © 2023 by Bellwether Media, Inc. BLASTOFF! READERS and associated logos are trademarks and/or registered trademarks of Bellwether Media, Inc.

Editor: Rebecca Sabelko   Series Design: Andrea Schneider   Book Designer: Laura Sowers

Printed in the United States of America, North Mankato, MN.

Table of Contents

What Is Camping?	4
Setting Up Camp	8
Camping Gear	14
Camping Safety	18
Glossary	22
To Learn More	23
Index	24

What Is Camping?

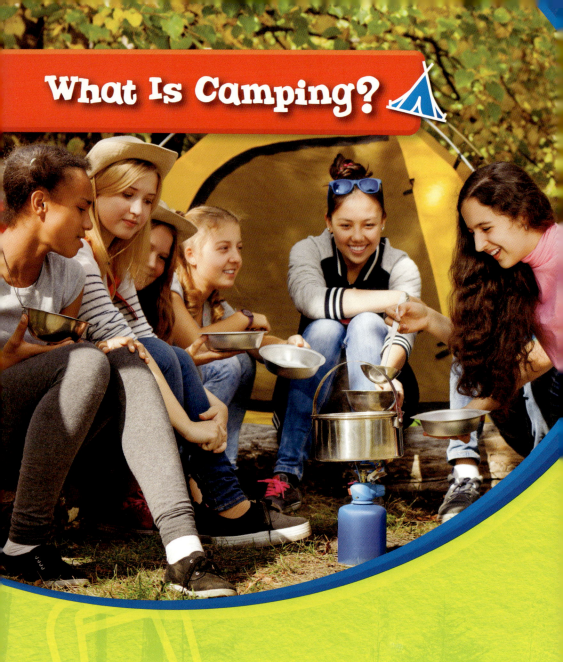

Camping is spending time living outdoors. Campers enjoy being in nature.

During the day, they might hike, fish, or swim.

fishing

At night, campers gather around a campfire. They eat and tell stories.

Favorite Camping Spot

Blackwoods Campground, Acadia National Park, Maine

Claim to Fame

- around 280 wooded campsites
- 10-minute hike to Atlantic Ocean
- running water

Some campers sleep under the stars in a tent. Others use different **shelters**.

Setting Up Camp

People can go tent, **RV**, or car camping. They choose a campsite that meets their needs.

Many campsites are in public **campgrounds**. Some are in wild areas.

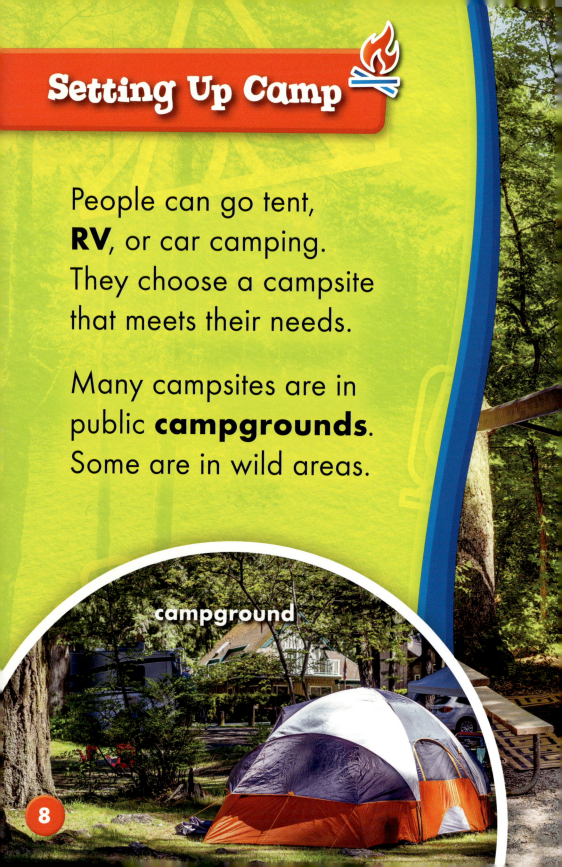

campground

Most people camp in tents. They find safe, dry ground.

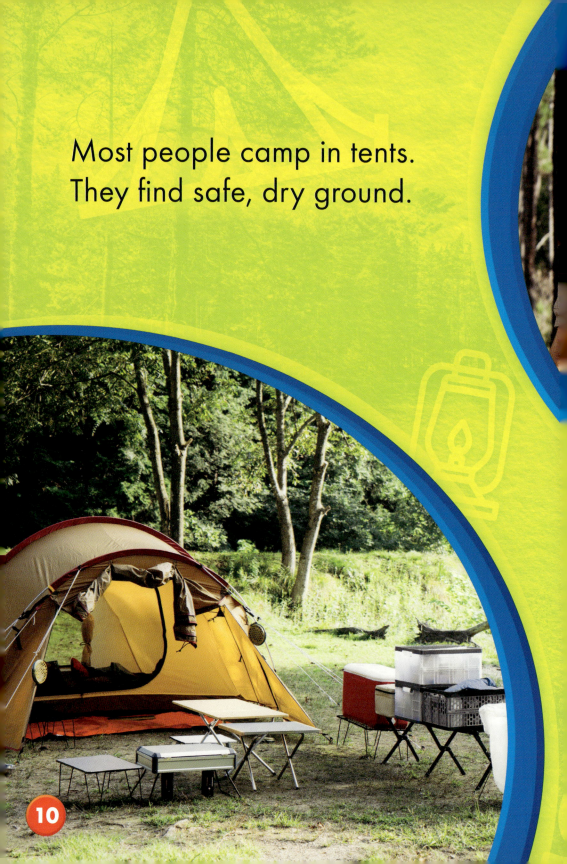

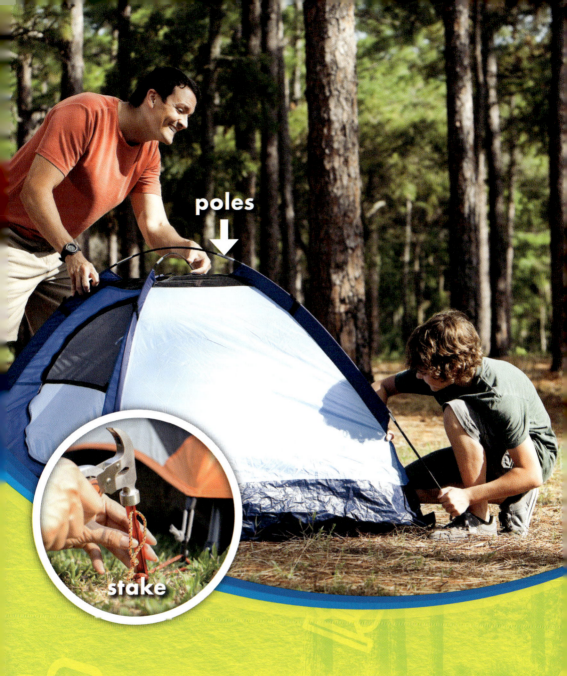

poles

stake

They slide poles through loops in the tent fabric. They **stake** tents to the ground.

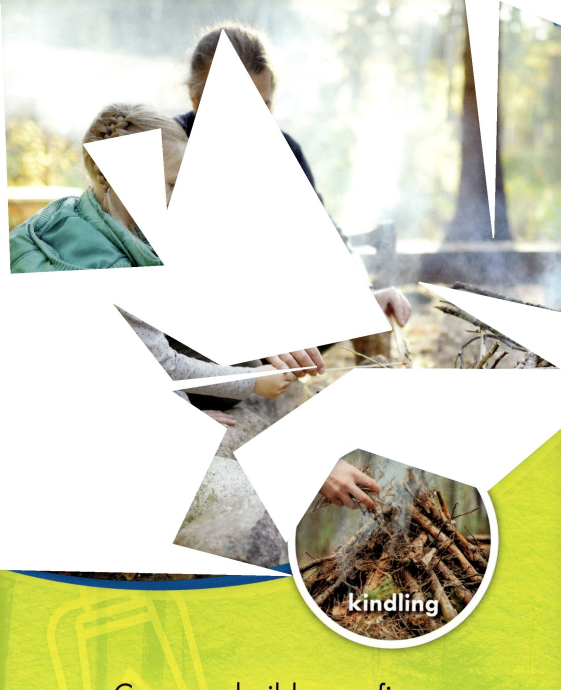

Campers build campfires. They collect **kindling** and wood.

Campfires are places to warm up, cook, or chat. Soon campers are ready to have fun!

Types of Campfires

teepee

lean-to

cross

log cabin

Camping Gear

Campers need **sturdy** shelters. Sleeping bags and pads make for cozy nights.

Campers must pack clothes for the weather. **Lanterns** are helpful when the sun goes down.

lantern

Campers need matches to start campfires. They must pack food, water, and dishes.

Camping Gear

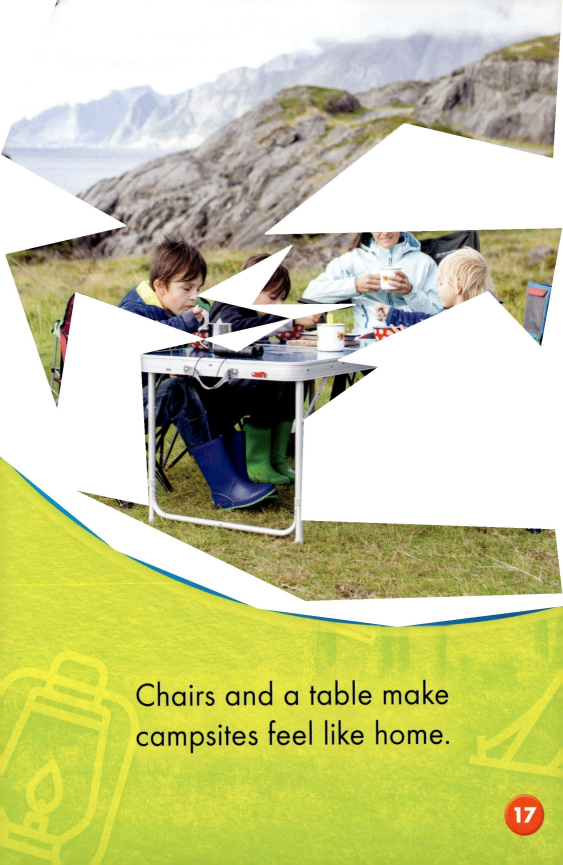

Chairs and a table make campsites feel like home.

Camping Safety

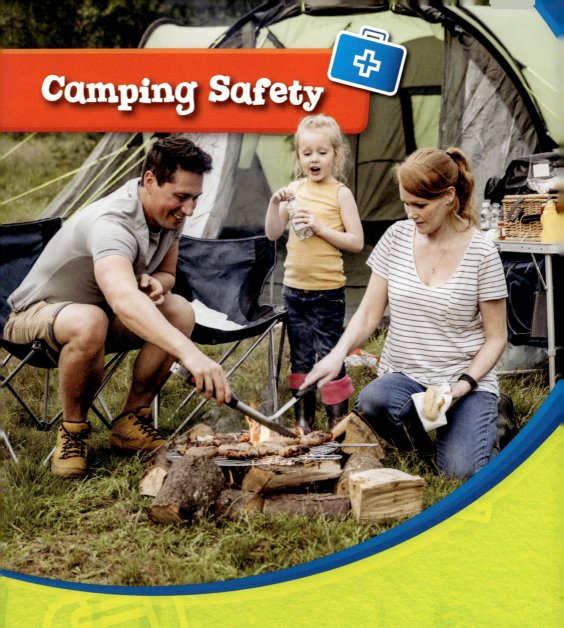

Campers must find safe campsites. They should stay clear of areas that flood.

Campers keep food packed away. They keep campfires under control.

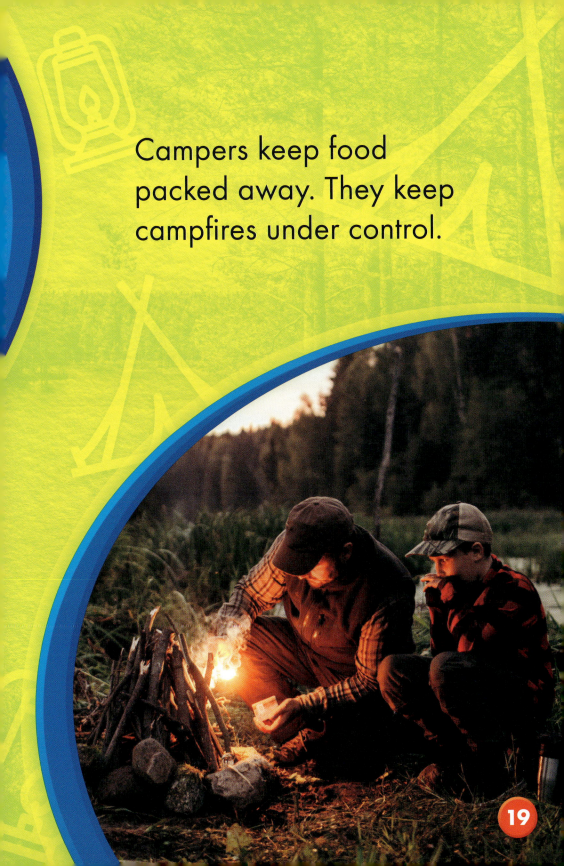

Campers carry maps and **first-aid kits** when they explore. They know what wild animals and plants are nearby.

Campers leave their campsites cleaner than they found them!

Glossary

campgrounds—large camping areas with many campsites; many campgrounds have bathrooms, water, and other services.

first-aid kits—emergency sets of supplies for treating sick or injured people

kindling—small pieces of wood, dried twigs, or sticks that easily catch fire but do not burn too quickly

lanterns—lights with handles for carrying

RV—recreational vehicle; RVs are like homes on wheels.

shelters—places that offer protection from weather and other dangers

stake—to fasten a tent to the ground by pounding in small metal posts called stakes

sturdy—strong

To Learn More

AT THE LIBRARY

Mann, Jennifer K. *The Camping Trip.* Somerville, Mass.: Candlewick Press, 2020.

Payne, Stefanie. *The National Parks: Discover All 62 Parks of the United States.* New York, N.Y.: DK Publishing, 2020.

Sumerak, Marc. *Survival Handbook: An Essential Companion to the Great Outdoors.* Bellevue, Wash.: Becker & Mayer! kids, 2019.

ON THE WEB

Factsurfer.com gives you a safe, fun way to find more information.

1. Go to www.factsurfer.com.
2. Enter "camping" into the search box and click 🔍.
3. Select your book cover to see a list of related content.

Index

animals, 20
campers, 4, 6, 7, 12, 13, 14, 16, 18, 19, 20, 21
campfire, 6, 7, 12, 13, 16, 19
campgrounds, 8
campsite, 8, 9, 17, 18, 21
car, 8
chairs, 17
clothes, 14
dishes, 16
favorite spot, 6
first-aid kits, 20
fish, 5
food, 16, 19
gear, 16
hike, 5
kindling, 12
lanterns, 14
maps, 20
matches, 16

nature, 4
pads, 14
plants, 20
RV, 8, 9
safety, 10, 18, 19, 20
shelters, 7, 14
sleeping bags, 14, 15
swim, 5
table, 17
tent, 7, 8, 10, 11
water, 16
wood, 12

The images in this book are reproduced through the courtesy of: Sergey Novikov, front cover, pp. 4-5; zealotPATT, p. 3; Jaren Jai Wicklund, p. 5; ScenincMedia, p. 6; anatoliy_gleb, pp. 6-7; Elena_Alex_Ferns, p. 8; dvande, pp. 8-9; Yagi-Studio, p. 10; kali9, pp. 10-11; Pentium5, p. 11; VALUA VITALY, p. 12; MNStudio, pp. 12-13; Olga Simonova, p. 14; Saturated, pp. 14-15; Alexlukin, p. 16 (tent); Olga Popova, p. 16 (lantern); candy candy, p. 16 (water); Anton Starikov, p. 16 (sleeping bag); Dan Thornberg, p. 16 (background); tatyana_tomsickova, pp. 16-17; JohnnyGreig, pp. 18-19; visualspace, p. 19; Leszek Glasner, p. 20; Air Images, pp. 20-21; Creativa Images, p. 22.